Published by

REARDON & SON
Publishers
CHELTENHAM, ENGLAND

Cotswold V

GW00703265

Copyright ⓒ

Reardon &

ISBN 0 9508674 0 3

Compiled, written and illustrated by
Nicholas A.P. Reardon
Peter T. Reardon
Printed
by
IN2PRINT Ltd
Cheltenham

1

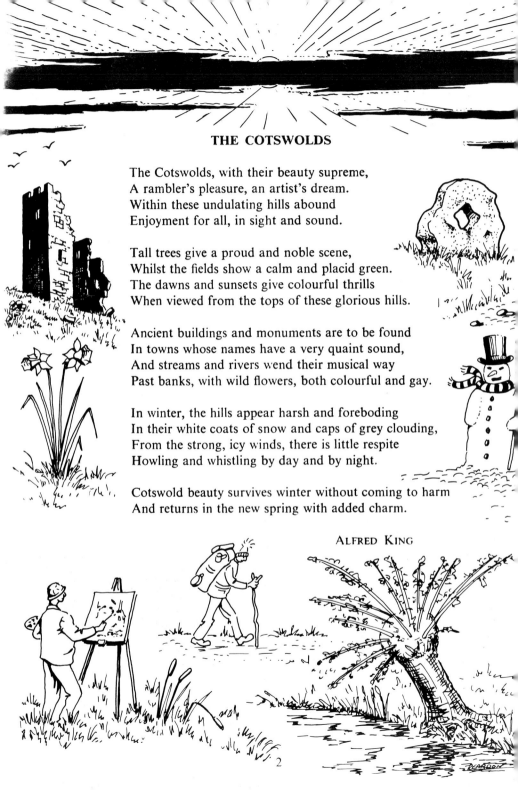

THE COTSWOLDS

The Cotswolds, with their beauty supreme,
A rambler's pleasure, an artist's dream.
Within these undulating hills abound
Enjoyment for all, in sight and sound.

Tall trees give a proud and noble scene,
Whilst the fields show a calm and placid green.
The dawns and sunsets give colourful thrills
When viewed from the tops of these glorious hills.

Ancient buildings and monuments are to be found
In towns whose names have a very quaint sound,
And streams and rivers wend their musical way
Past banks, with wild flowers, both colourful and gay.

In winter, the hills appear harsh and foreboding
In their white coats of snow and caps of grey clouding,
From the strong, icy winds, there is little respite
Howling and whistling by day and by night.

Cotswold beauty survives winter without coming to harm
And returns in the new spring with added charm.

ALFRED KING

The Cotswolds

The Cotswolds today offers more for the visitor than in days gone by. There are shops of all kinds, places for refreshment, amusement and interest. Long and short stay accommodation is available in most areas, and is never very far from some historical house, monument or archeological site. Many of these sites are where men some 4-5000 years ago lived, raised their families and buried their dead. They lived at a pace compatible with nature, evolution and survival of the species. They travelled and hunted at speeds that suited man or animal in the struggle for survival.

In present times, with our Space Age Technology, Interplanetary Flights, Space Stations and Satelite Communications being in every-day use, distances described in Light Years is not uncommon. It's all so big. It's all so complicated. But, with all those wonderful things going on around us, there is still gratification in being able to stop and visit some of these legacies of the past and let our mind travel back in time. Standing quietly on the site of an ancient Stone or Iron Age camp, it is almost possible to hear the sounds of life as it was in those far off days. With the help of this little book it is hoped you will attain a greater appreciation of some of these historic monuments, if only by the fact that you reached it in the same way as our forefathers did - on foot.

If you have enjoyed this little publication, it may create a new interest for you and, through not travelling so great a distance, a more intimate knowledge of the Cotswolds may have been achieved.

Peter T Reardon

Leckhampton
Cheltenham Spa
1983

It is not suggested that special equipment or clothing is required for the walks described in this book, but suitable clothing would be well advised. Depending on earlier weather conditions it could be very muddy in places. It could also be cold, if the wind is blowing across wet land. So stout footwear and windproof or waterproof (in case of rain) outer clothes. If it is warm and sunny in the valley it could still be fairly cool on the hills. Remember, you are walking at about 700-1000ft above sea level in some places and probably very exposed, and you could be the first obstruction the wind has found since leaving the Atlantic. So, some strong shoes, and warm but lightweight clothing should be the order of the day.

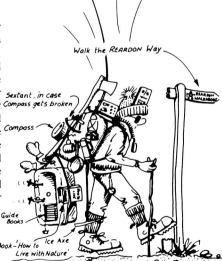

Walk the REARDON Way

Sextant, in case Compass gets broken

Compass

Guide Books

Book-'How to Live with Nature'

Ice Axe

The Rollright Stones Walkabout

This is not a walkabout as such but because these stones are an important part of the Cotswolds it would not be right to leave them out. A suggestion would be to park your car in one of the parking places, then visit the Ring of Stones first and the King Stone across the road next. An amusing little point here, you have now walked from Oxfordshire to Warwickshire! Then walk on up the road turn right, as shown on the map, along the side of the field with the hedge and fence on your left. You will then arrive at the Whispering Knights. Legend has it that a witch met a King and his army whose intention it was to rule the whole of England. The witch did not like this very much, so she made a bargain with him that if he take seven long strides and 'if Long compton thou cans't see, King of England thou shalt be'. This was too much for the King's vanity - but after the seventh long stride he could still not see Long Compton and he and his men were all turned to stone. Why were the Whispering Knights so far away? Ah! treachery was afoot here. They intended to overthrow the King when he had taken all England and didn't want anyone to overhear their plan. That's how the legend goes, but it is in fact, more likely to be as the little plaque describes in front of the Circle, a Bronze Age stone circle for ritual purposes dating back some 3500 years. It is very old for sure, and some amusement can be had trying to count the number of stones in the circle, as it is claimed that the same number can never be counted twice. All the Stones are now a National Monument and are in the care of the Department of the Environment. Contrary to much general thinking, the Rollright Stones are not in Gloucestershire, though they are as much a part of the Cotswolds as Chipping Campden, Cirencester and Stow on the Wold. The Circle and Whispering Knights are in Oxfordshire while the King Stone, just across the road, is in Warwickshire. Long Compton lies about a mile north of the Rollright Stones.

There is a story that tells of the King, the Whispering Knights and all the Army going down the hill to drink the water from a spring on New Years Day.

4

The ROLLRIGHT STONES
Walkabout

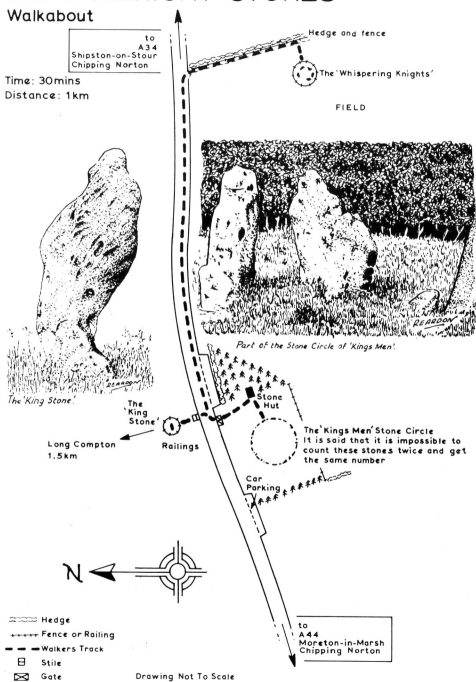

to
A34
Shipston-on-Stour
Chipping Norton

Time: 30mins
Distance: 1km

Hedge and fence

The 'Whispering Knights'

FIELD

Part of the Stone Circle of 'Kings Men'.

The 'King Stone'.

The 'King Stone'

Stone Hut

The 'Kings Men' Stone Circle
It is said that it is impossible to
count these stones twice and get
the same number

Long Compton
1.5km

Railings

Car Parking

N

Hedge
Fence or Railing
Walkers Track
Stile
Gate

Drawing Not To Scale

to
A44
Moreton-in-Marsh
Chipping Norton

The Nibley Knoll Walkabout

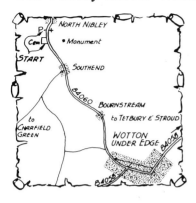

(1) Park at either point A or B. Point A is by a cemetery and B is by a telephone box. (2) Cross the road (B4060) and start to walk up the lane opposite (The lane is almost opposite the cemetery). At the entrance to the lane, on the left, is a sign explaining where a key to the Monument can be obtained locally, and on the right, is a sign pointing to the 'Cotswold Way, Wotton Hill 2km and Wotton under Edge 3km'. Follow Yellow Arrows (FYA). (3)On up the lane you will see on your right a path, now closed. This was the old way up to the Tyndale Monument. Ignore this path and keep walking (4) until you see a Yellow Arrow on a tree to your left. FYA. (If you reach a gate you have missed the arrow, see map). Climb path on your right and follow it until (5) it leads to a section of fence with an arrow on it. FYA. Climb over fence, veer right and follow path up to the Monument. (6) Excellent views can be seen from the bottom of the Monument over the Severn Valley to the North, West and South. Now start walking to a nearby stone, following the wire fence (see map). The stone (7) is a Topograph. (8) Keep following the fence, passing a stone seat with an arrow on it. FYA. (9) As you pass through some trees you will see a gate with an arrow on it. FYA over gate. There are now several paths leading in different directions, so take the right hand path. At (10) you should see a wooden fence to your right and several paths leading off to your left. Ignore these paths, even the one which has a Yellow Arrow pointing along it, and keep straight on. (11) The path you are now on will take you all round the spur of the hill, on top of which is the tree covered Brackenbury Ditches Hill Fort. (12) On the way round you should be able to have a good view of the Monument to your right. (13) Keep following the same path (this can be muddy in wet weather) (14) until you come to a path on your left. At this point you should see a tree with a Yellow Arrow pointing along this path. FYA, and turn left along this path. You will now be following arrows all the way back to the start. (15) When path forks, FYA and take right fork. (16) On your left you will see large banks and ditches. These were the outside defences of the Hill Fort. This section can be extremely muddy in bad weather. (17) You will now come to a 'cross-roads' of paths (see map). FYA and take the one with the Yellow Arrow pointing down it, (18) and keep following this path until you come out onto the major path between (10) and (11). Turn right and keep on this path, ignoring all turnings on your right. You will now come back to the gate at (9). From here you just retrace your steps back to the starting point via the Topograph, Monument and lane.

The Tyndale Monument was erected on Nibley Knoll in 1866 in memory of William Tyndale, translater of the New Testament into English. He went to Germany to prepare his translation, published it in 1535 and was burnt at the stake for heresy the following year.

The Topograph was erected in 1977 by the people of North Nibley to commemorate the Silver Jubilee of Her Majesty Queen Elizabeth II.

Brackenbury Ditches is an Iron Age Hill Fort dating back up to 2,500 years ago and covering about 5½ acres overall.

6

NIBLEY KNOLL & BRACKENBURY DITCHES

To North Nibley

Walkabout

Time: 1 hr 20 mins
Distance: 4 km

Sign to say where key to
Monument can be obtained

④ Yellow Arrow pointing Right
FYA

Cemetery

① Steep Path

② ③ Stile FYA ⑤

Sign to
Cotswold Way
Wotton Hill 2km
Wotton under
Edge 3km

Parking

⑥ Tyndale Monument

Views

NIBLEY KNOLL

⑦ Topograph

B4060
To
Wotton under Edge

Views

⑧ Stone Seat
FYA

Views

⑨ Gateway with
Arrow
FYA

The Monument to William Tyndale

N

⑩ ⑱
FYA

⑰ FYA

⑪ BRACKENBURY DITCHES

⑫ ⑯

⑮ Arrow on
tree
FYA

HILL FORT

FYA

⑬ ⑭

✗+++ Track now Closed

FYA Follow Yellow Arrows

⊟ Stile

⊠ Farm Type Gate

==‒== Tracks and Bridlepaths

+++++ Fence

‒ ‒ ‒ Walkers Track

This Drawing is Not To Scale

7

The Crickley Hill Country Park Walkabout

(1) Turn into the Park from the B4070 and proceed up the drive to the car parks. Park in either one. If you have parked in the large one, to start the walk (2) go through the small car park, opposite the Wardens Office/Toilets, and (3) climb steps in the corner of the car park up to the track and turn right. You will be Following Yellow Arrows (FYA) from now until (12). In a few paces you will come to a gate and a stile. (4) Climb over the stile on your left FYA towards the trees. Excellent views can be seen on your left. (6) FYA into woods. (7) Follow the path through woods. If path splits, take major path. Minor paths should rejoin at (8) anyway. (8) Path comes out by a stone wall on your right, and a post with an arrow on it pointing along a path which runs parallel to a fence. FYA. (9) Continue walking, always keeping the fence on your right. (10) Climb over stile. (11) Continue walking. You will now have a wood on your right. (12) At the end of the path, climb over stile, down steps on to the road (can be slippery if the weather is, or has been wet) and turn right. (You will notice across the road there is a sign pointing in the direction from where you have come, saying 'Public Footpath, Crickley Hill 1'). (13) Almost immediately on your right, you will come to a gate with a blue arrow on it leading into the wood you were just walking beside. Go through the gate and Follow Blue Arrows. You are now on a bridleway, so it can be a bit muddy. (14) The bridleway goes up the opposite side of the fence you followed down, so now walk keeping the fence on your right. (15) Keep walking until your path is forced left by a stone wall. Now walk on keeping the wall on your right and the wood on your left. (16) This path ends with a gate on your right and to your left, over the field by some buildings, you should be able to see a Long Barrow with trees on it. The gate on your right is a weighted gate of 56lbs. Go through the gate (17) and walk along the side of the field keeping the fence on your left. (18) Go through the next gateway you come to. Now keep fence on your right (19) until you reach the main road (B4070). Turn right and keep walking, until you reach the entrance to the Park into which you originally drove. Walk up the drive and back to your car.

The Hill Fort on the promontary of Crickley Hill is indeed, a super defensive position. It is triangular in shape with an eath rampart and ditch across the eastern side and steep natural slopes on the north-west and south-west sides. There is evidence of a settlement here about 5000 years or more ago, with what is visible today is mostly from Iron Age days. A viewing platform has been built so that much of the site can be seen from there. A number of illustrated information panels have been erected telling the story of the archaeology and geology of the site. There is also some evidence of Roman occupation in the area.

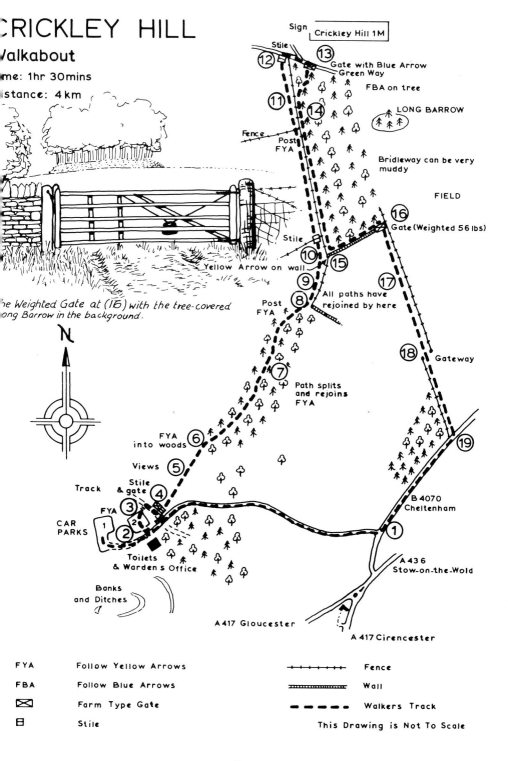

CRICKLEY HILL

Walkabout

Time: 1hr 30mins

Distance: 4km

Sign [Crickley Hill 1M]

Stile

(12) (13)
Gate with Blue Arrow
Green Way

FBA on tree

(11) (14)

LONG BARROW

Fence

Post
FYA

Bridleway can be very
muddy

FIELD

(16)
Gate (Weighted 56 lbs)

Stile

(10) (15)

Yellow Arrow on wall

(9)

(17)

The Weighted Gate at (16) with the tree-covered
Long Barrow in the background.

Post
FYA

(8)
All paths have
rejoined by here

(18)
Gateway

(7)
Path splits
and rejoins
FYA

N

FYA
into woods (6)

Views (5)

(19)

Stile
& gate (4)

Track

FYA (3)

CAR
PARKS 1 2

(2)

B 4070
Cheltenham

(1)

Toilets
& Wardens Office

A436
Stow-on-the-Wold

Banks
and Ditches

A417 Gloucester

A 417 Cirencester

FYA	Follow Yellow Arrows		Fence
FBA	Follow Blue Arrows		Wall
⊠	Farm Type Gate		Walkers Track
⊟	Stile		This Drawing is Not To Scale

9

The Belas Knap Walkabout

If this walk is approached from the Cheltenham or Winchcombe direction (1) drive up Corndean Lane and when the road forks left and right, take the left fork and then park in the layby just on your left. (2) Across the road from where you are now parked you will see a gate and stile with a yellow arrow on it, and a sign pointing to Belas Knapp. Follow Yellow Arrow (FYA). Go through the gate or over the stile and climb up the path (can be very muddy) (3) until you come to a gate. FYA. Go on through the gate and turn left, keeping the wall and fence to your left. (4) At the corner of the field turn right. FYA, keeping the stone wall to your left, (good views across the country can be seen from this stretch) (5) until you come to a gate and a sign. FYA though gate into the next field, keeping the wall and then trees to your left (fine views may be seen from here on a clear day). (6) You have now arrived at Belas Knap Long Barrow. After you have looked round Belas Knap, leave by the stone stile on the opposite side of the site to the one you used on your arrival (see map). (7) Walk along the edge of the field keeping the stone wall to your right. (8) This track comes out into a lane. Turn right and FYA through gateposts and down the lane (9) passing through Hill Barn Farm on the way (good views towards Winchcombe, Sudeley Castle, Toddington Manor and Evesham are possible on a clear day). (10) When the lane is joined by another lane from the left, FYA on tree on right and keep right until the lane joins a road. (11) Turn right here and walk back to your car.

The mound of Belas Knap is just over 54m long, 18m wide at its widest part and 4m high. Some of the finds are in the Cheltenham Museum. The monument is in the care of the Department of the Environment, and leaflets describing it can be obtained from the Hailes Abbey site (N.T.), also in the care of the Department of the Environment, on the north side of Winchcombe on the A46 Broadway road.

BELAS KNAP from the SOUTH

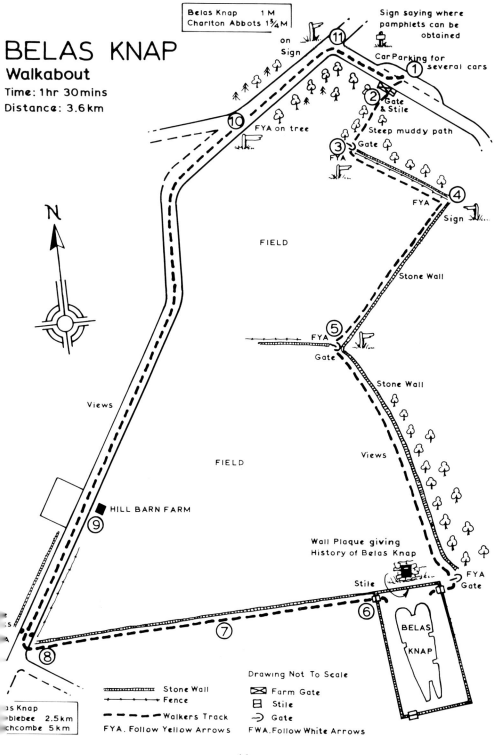

BELAS KNAP
Walkabout
Time: 1hr 30mins
Distance: 3.6km

Belas Knap 1 M
Charlton Abbots 1¾M
on Sign

Sign saying where pamphlets can be obtained

Car Parking for several cars

① ② Gate & Stile

Steep muddy path

⑪

⑩ FYA on tree

③ Gate
FYA

FYA
④ Sign

FIELD

Stone Wall

⑤ FYA
Gate

Stone Wall

Views

FIELD

Views

Wall Plaque giving History of Belas Knap

HILL BARN FARM
⑨

FYA Gate

Stile
⑥

BELAS KNAP

⑦

⑧

s Knap
:s
A

as Knap
:blebee 2.5km
chcombe 5km

N

Drawing Not To Scale

Stone Wall
Fence
Walkers Track
FYA. Follow Yellow Arrows

Farm Gate
Stile
Gate
FWA.Follow White Arrows

11

The Coopers Hill Walkabout

On arriving at the start of the walk on Coopers Hill (1) park in car parks A, B or C (as shown on the map). There is a walk-way between the car park A and B. (2) The walk starts from car park B and a lot of it follows the Cotswold Way. (The Cotswold Way is a 100 mile walk following the Cotswold escarpment as closely as possible). Just by the public convenience is a map of the Nature Trail and some steps. Climb steps (3) and follow the sign to the viewpoint (4). Excellent views can be obtained from here on a clear day. (5) Now walk back down to (3) again and follow the sign pointing along the Nature Trail. You will be following Blue Posts and Yellow Arrows. On the way you will see a Blue Notice and this will tell you a little about the area you are now in. (6) Keep on following the Blue Posts. There will be a point where the path splits and Blue Posts go to the right and Yellow Arrows go to the left. Either one of the paths can be taken as they rejoin again later. (7) When you reach a fence the Posts will be Brown and you will see another Notice saying a little about this area. (8) Follow the Brown Posts until they give way to an Orange Post and Notice, again describing the area. Continue by following these (9) until they in turn change to Black Posts. Continue following the Black Posts until you emerge from the woods. (10) At this point you should be able to see the famous May Pole, and (11) the section of the hill that is used for Whitson Bank Holiday Cheese Rolling. Splendid views can be seen from here towards Cheltenham and the north. You are now standing 850 feet above sea level. (12) Now continue following the Black Posts until they (13) in turn change to Yellow Posts. (14) Follow the Yellow Posts, but after a while these will be replaced by Red Posts and at this point (15) you will be very close to the Cross-ridge Dyke. There is not a lot left of the Dyke today, but some remains can be seen. It is believed to date back to Iron Age days and may be connected in some way with possible Iron Age earthworks on High Brotheridge, just south of this walk. (16) Follow the Red Posts until they also change, this time to Green Posts. (17) This Green Section will take you back to the start of the Orange Section at (8). At this point turn left and retrace your steps back along first the Brown Section and then the Blue, until you arrive back at the car park B.

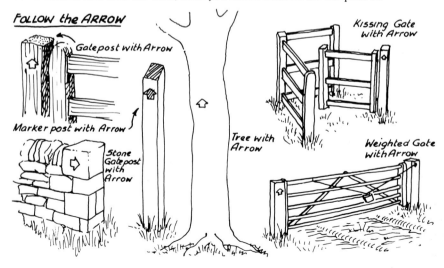

COOPERS HILL
Walkabout

Time: 1 hr 30mins
Distance: 3.5 km

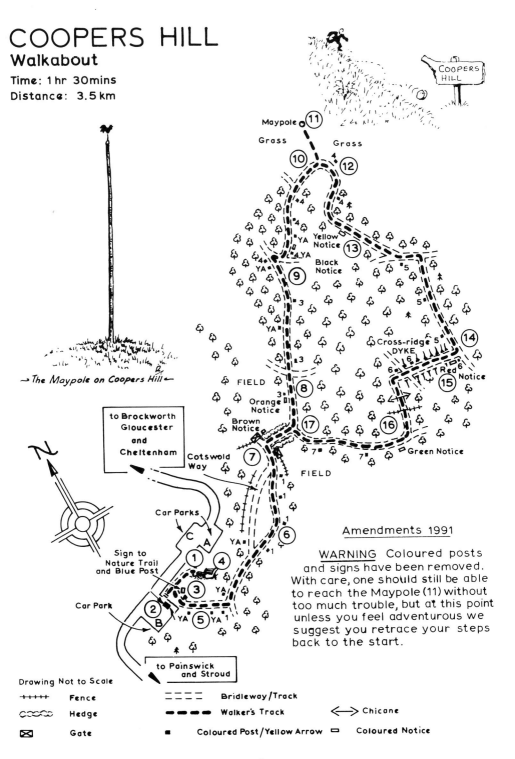

The Maypole on Coopers Hill

Amendments 1991

WARNING Coloured posts and signs have been removed. With care, one should still be able to reach the Maypole (11) without too much trouble, but at this point unless you feel adventurous we suggest you retrace your steps back to the start.

Drawing Not to Scale

+++++	Fence	
∞∞∞∞	Hedge	
⊠	Gate	

＝＝＝	Bridleway/Track	
━ ━ ━	Walker's Track	⟷ Chicane
■	Coloured Post/Yellow Arrow	▭ Coloured Notice

The Tunnel House (The Round House) Walkabout

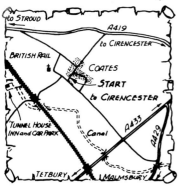

(1) After leaving the A419 or A433 park somewhere in the village of Coates. The road marked on the map usually has good parking places. You can also start this walk from (4) Tunnel House, but you will have to ask permission first to use their car park. To start the walk you leave the village by the road sign-posted 'Tarlton 1, Rodmarton 2' (see map). Keep walking along this road, going under the bridge, until you come to a lane on your right - just before a bridge over - marked with a pub sign 'Tunnel House'. Turn right down this lane and keep walking (4) until you reach Tunnel House. At the time of writing, hot and cold food and coffee was available during opening times, and this can make a pleasant break in the walk. (5) Just off the car park in the SE corner, you will find a path leading to the canal. Follow this path down to the canal tunnel entrance. (6) Keeping the canal to your left, start walking along the bank of the canal and (7) under the road bridge. (8) Soon you will come to a 'tower like building'. This is a Round House. After looking round the Round House (9) continue walking, passing next, under a railway bridge. (10) The next bridge you come to climb up the bank on your right, cross over the bridge and go through the farm gate, passing a building on your right. (11) Now continue across field keeping stone wall to your right. (12) At the end of this field you will find a stone stile (13), climb over the stile and cross next field keeping stone wall to your left. (14) At the end of this field climb over stone stile and turn left along the road. (15) The first turning on your right will lead you back to (1). (16) The first turning on your left will start you off at (2) again.

The canal you have followed in this walk is a small section of the Severn and Thames Canal, which has been derelict for many years now. During the upsurge in interest in the canal system for pleasure boating, the Portal of the Coates end of the tunnel has been renewed. This was carried out by local craftsmen in 1977 and unveiled by Earl Bathurst. When the canal was built the tunnel from Coates to Sapperton was the longest in the country, being $2\frac{1}{4}$ miles long. The canal today, is in the care of the Stroudwater, Thames and Severn Canal Trust and the restoration comes under their control. The Round Houses as seen at (8) (though habitable), were used by the lengthsmen on the canal and were built at set distances along the route. At these points the men on the barges had to pay a toll to the lengthsman before he could proceed. The tolls collected helped to pay for the upkeep of the canal, often undertaken by the lengthsman. These men lived and raised their families in these Round Houses; it was their home.

Another item of interest, about a quarter of a mile to the right of, or south of (10) where this walk turns left over the bridge, there is Trewsbury Hill Fort, an Iron Age Camp. Most of the ditches and ramparts are still discernable. The possibility of Roman occupation is supported by the finding of a few Roman remains. The Camp is on private property and is therefore not open to the public.

"Legging it" through a Canal Tunnel.

TUNNEL HOUSE (& The ROUND HOUSE)

Walkabout

Time: 1hr 30mins
Distance: 4.5km

Tunnel House
Car Park

5
4

Cirencester
Park
Gate

6

7

Pub Sign
'Tunnel
House'

3

8

The Round House

Tunnel Entrance
after its restoration
in 1977

Bridge over carrying
operational British
Rail trackway

9

N

A Round House. Once the homes
of the lengthmen, who collected
the tolls on the S&T Canal.

The Severn & Thames Canal

Signpost to
Coates Church
Stroud 10

Tarlton 1
Rodmarton 2

Kemble
Cirencester
A433

16

2

Parking
along this
road

15

1

Stone Wall

Gate and Stile

10

Barn

12

11

Stile

Bridge over Canal

Farm
Building

13

Stone Stile

14

Stile

Symbols are as
other pages

This Drawing is Not to Scale

15

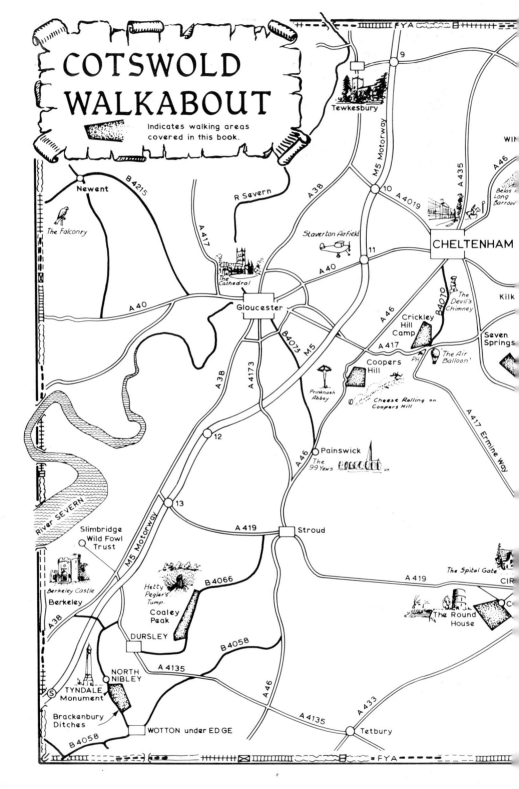

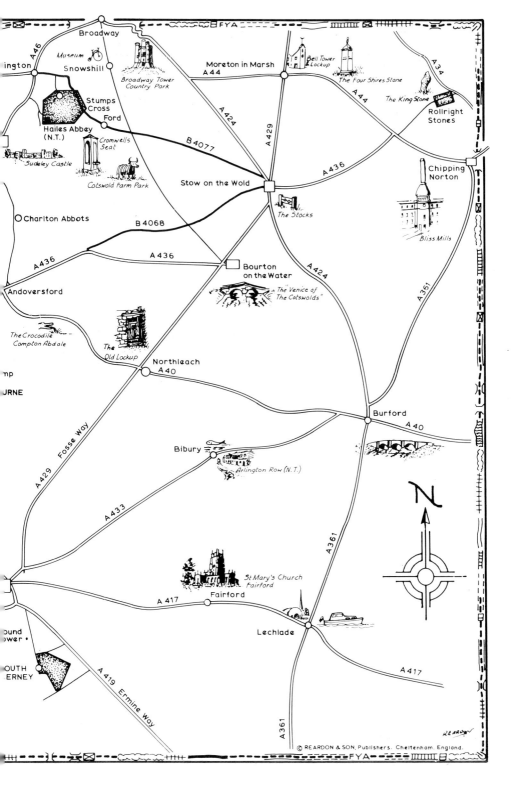

The Norbury Camp Walkabout

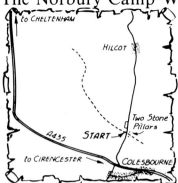

This walk starts part way up a minor road from the main A435 near Colesbourne, signposted to Hilcot and Kilkenny. About half a mile up this road, past Southbury Farm, will be found two large stone gate posts on the right at a point where woods start on the left. A bridleway/track goes straight across the road here. There is parking just a little further up the road, on the left. (1) Walk back to the track, if you have parked off the road (see map). Start walking down the track (2) passing a large barn on your right. (3) You will have trees to your right and fields to your left. (4) Next you will come to a crossroads of tracks just as the trees run out on your right and start again on your left. At this point turn right (see map) and follow the track (5) up the field, keeping the trees to your right and the field to your left. (6) Keep following this track as it bends round the field to the left. (7) You will now have a hedge/fence/wall on your right. (8) This track now takes you through a clump of trees marking the site of Norbury Camp. Along the line of trees off to the right will be seen banks and ditches which formed part of the defences when the camp was in use about 2500 years ago. Most of them have been lost probably due to cultivation of the land. (9) After you have passed over Norbury Camp you will come to a track off to your right. Ignore this one and keep going along major track. (10) This will take you to a gateway which you go through and walk on. (11) This track now joins another track by a small house. Turn left here and follow the new track. (12) This track is joined by another coming in from the right. When the tracks meet, keep straight on. (13) You can now follow the track you are on back to the start, and your car.

The Cottage at (11)

18

NORBURY CAMP
Walkabout

Time: 1hr 40mins
Distance: 4 km

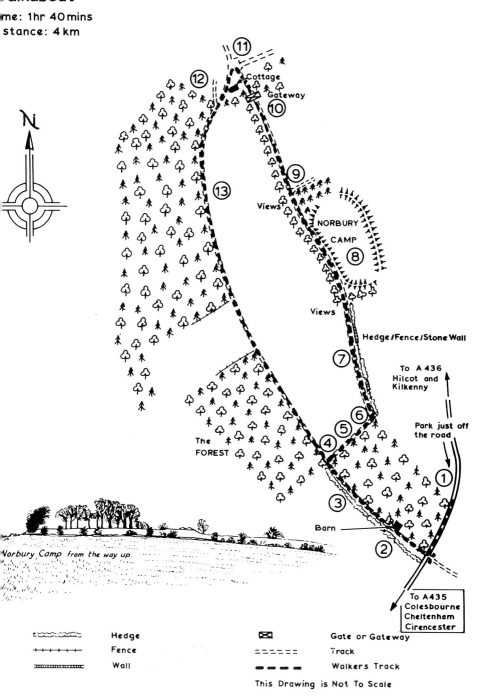

N

Cottage
Gateway
Views
NORBURY
CAMP
Views
Hedge/Fence/Stone Wall

To A436
Hilcot and
Kilkenny

Park just off
the road

The
FOREST

Barn

Norbury Camp from the way up.

To A435
Colesbourne
Cheltenham
Cirencester

	Hedge		⋈	Gate or Gateway
	Fence		═ ═ ═ ═	Track
	Wall		▬ ▬ ▬ ▬	Walkers Track

This Drawing is Not To Scale

19

The Coaley Peak Walkabout

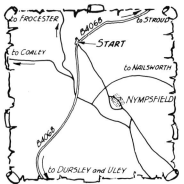

(1) Park your car in the car park near the public conveniences. Walk up past Nympsfield Long Barrow (2), through the gate, along the edge of the field and then through the next gate to View Point (3). Follow Yellow Arrow (4) through the woods and on to the road. (5) Turn left and go to the cross roads, then turn right. Next, take the bridleway (6) on the right marked with signpost pointing to 'Uley Bury 1.5km, Dursley 5km, Cam 5km.' Follow the path downhill to the bottom. The path splits into three on the way down, but by taking the middle or right-hand paths you will be going the correct way. (7) You will come out into a lane with houses in it. Turn left here and then left again into the first path on your left (see map). Ignore turn-offs like the one you have immediately on your right and continue on up through the woods. This path takes you to the main road (B4066) at (8). For a shorter walk you should now read from (14). If you prefer the longer walk take the path (bridleway) which runs adjacent to the main road and continue until the path forks left and right. Take the left fork (9) following the hill round (see map) (10), (11) and (12) always keeping the fence on your right. You are now walking round the famous Uley Bury Hill Fort. It is believed to be the finest of its kind in the country. Superb views are obtainable from (11) and (12) on the way round, both viewpoints being 700 feet above sea level. Go through the gate (13) (which was the right fork of (9)) and away back down to the road (14). Turn left when you get on to the road. Walk along road (15). At (16) the key to Hetty Peglers Tump is obtainable from the house for a very small charge per person. Just here on the opposite side of the road, is a small promontary called West Hill, just above the 800ft level. There is evidence that there was a camp here from early British (the Dobunni Tribe) and Roman times. (17) Hetty Peglers Tump is visible from the road and quite easy to reach. The path to it leads along the edge of a field and you leave by the same way. (18) Continue along the road in the same direction as before and go straight over the road junction, following the B4066 Stroud Road. (19) When you come to the Coaley Peak Picnic Area, turn left and follow the path back to the car park at (1).

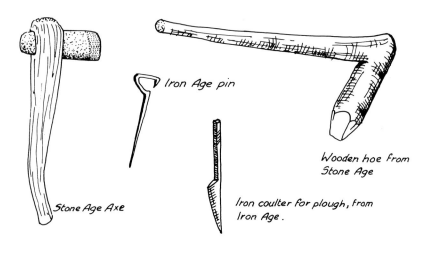

Iron Age pin

Wooden hoe from Stone Age

Stone Age Axe

Iron coulter for plough, from Iron Age.

COALEY PEAK

Walkabout

Time: 2 hrs 30 mins

Distance: 7.5 km

Ammendments 1991

(6) A new sign has replaced the old one which now has a Blue Arrow with a White Dot to indicate the Bridleway.

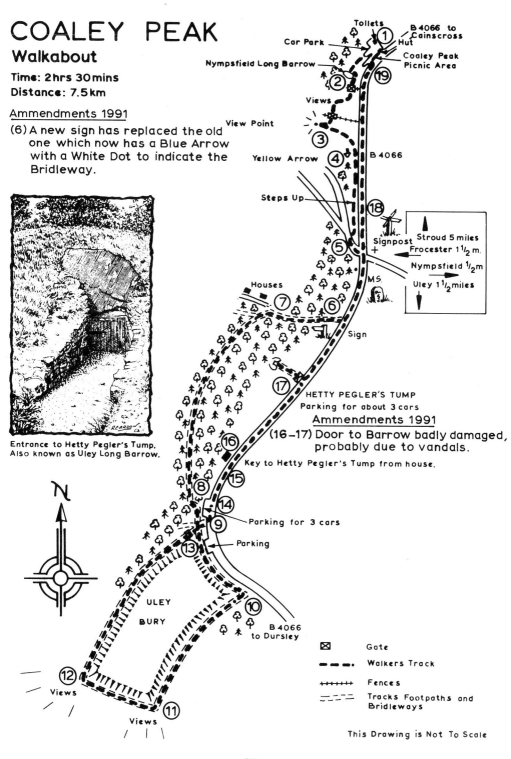

Entrance to Hetty Pegler's Tump. Also known as Uley Long Barrow.

Toilets

B 4066 to Cainscross

Car Park

Hut

Cooley Peak Picnic Area

Nympsfield Long Barrow

Views

View Point

Yellow Arrow

B 4066

Steps Up

Signpost

Stroud 5 miles
Frocester 1½ m.
Nympsfield ½ m
Uley 1½ miles

Houses

M.S.

Sign

HETTY PEGLER'S TUMP
Parking for about 3 cars

Ammendments 1991

(16–17) Door to Barrow badly damaged, probably due to vandals.

Key to Hetty Pegler's Tump from house.

Parking for 3 cars

Parking

ULEY

BURY

B 4066 to Dursley

Views

Views

Views

N

	Gate
⊠	Gate
● ─ ─ ●	Walkers Track
+++++++	Fences
═ ─ ─ ═	Tracks Footpaths and Bridleways

This Drawing is Not To Scale

21

The South Cerney Walkabout

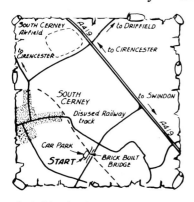

(1) Park in the car park just behind the brick built bridge. (2) To start this walk go through gateway in the corner of the car park and walk along the old dismantled railway track (3) until you come to (4) a stile on your right. Go over the stile and turn left along main road (5) and start walking into South Cerney. (6) Just after a road on the right named The Lennards, you will see a Footpath sign, next to a bus stop, leading over a small bridge. (7) Follow this footpath on through two kissing gates until you come to another bridge. (8) Go over the bridge and into the lane. Now turn left (9) and follow the lane until it joins a main road. On the way you will have the River Churn on your left and your right, as the river splits just the other side of the bridge in Silver Street. Also on your right, you will see in a garden a small tower. (10) When the lane joins the main road (Silver St.), turn right and (11) keep walking out of South Cerney until you come to a road on your right (12), the sign pointing down this road says 'Diffield 2 and Cricklade'. Turn down this road (13) and walk on until you come to Footpath signs on both sides of the road. Take the right hand footpath through the gate. (14) You are now following a disused canal and will be until (17). Keeping the canal to your left, walk on. (15) When you come to a gate leading onto a road go through the gate, cross the road to start on the footpath again. (16) Just past some old wooden lock gates the track has a right turn to Crane Farm. Ignore this turning and walk straight on keeping the canal on your left. (17) Now keep walking until you come to an old ruin on your left, on the other bank of the canal, by a bridge. (18) At this point take the stile on your right and start walking at right angles to the canal (see map). (19) Here you will have a fence to your left and bushes to your right to start this track. (20) This will change as you go along and sometimes you will have water on both sides of your path. When you come to a fence blocking the track, climb over the fence and keep walking on, in the same direction. (21) this trail ends with a gate. Ignore the gate and go over the stile on your left (22) into G.X. Fisheries car park. Now cross bridge into Horseshoe Lane. (23) Follow lane over bridge and past the Rainbow Lake on your right until it joins Robert Franklin Way and main road into South Cerney. (24) Join main road and turn left. You are now near (5) and should easily be able to retrace your steps back to the car park.

The disused canal that you have been walking alongside from (14) to (17) was part of the Severn and Thames Canal. This canal was built during the late 1700's and was completed in 1789. This enabled much heavy freight to be carried at a cheaper rate than on roads or rail. It was, unfortunately, bought by the G.W.R. and closed in 1893. There is, today, a much greater interest in the waterways system, mainly for pleasure boating, but we could see some revival of goods being carried on the canals again, as and when sections are renovated.

SOUTH CERNEY

Walkabout

Time: 2 hrs 30mins
Distance: 8.25km

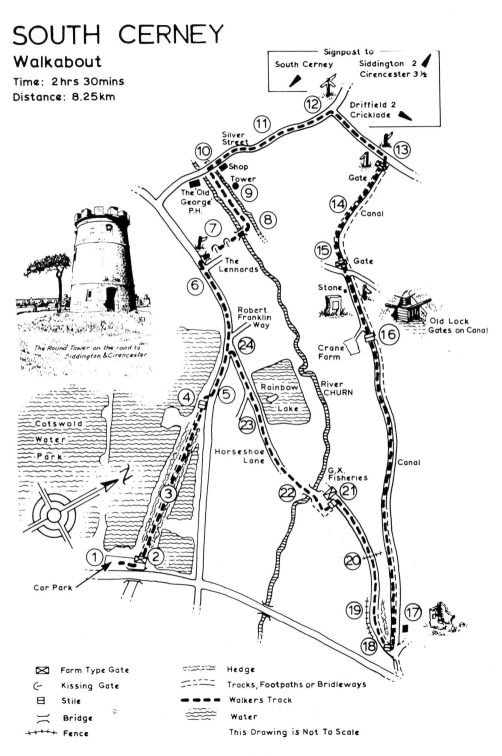

Signpost to —
South Cerney   Siddington 2
Cirencester 3½

Driffield 2
Cricklade

Silver Street

Shop
Tower
The 'Old George' P.H.

The Lennards

Robert Franklin Way

Gate

Canal

Gate

Stone

Old Lock Gates on Canal

Crane Farm

Rainbow Lake

River CHURN

Cotswold Water Park

Horseshoe Lane

G.X. Fisheries

Canal

Car Park

The Round Tower on the road to
Siddington & Cirencester

⊠	Farm Type Gate	⌒⌒⌒ Hedge
⌐	Kissing Gate	‑‑‑‑ Tracks, Footpaths or Bridleways
日	Stile	■ ■ ■ Walkers Track
⌒	Bridge	⌒⌒⌒ Water
┼┼┼┼	Fence	This Drawing is Not To Scale

23

The Stumps Cross to Hailes Abbey Walkabout

(1) Park by Stumps Cross or across the road in lane as shown on the map. To start the walk (2) take the farm road by the Cross that is sign-posted 'Bridleway to Farmcote 2.5km, Hailes Abbey 3km, Winchcombe 6km'. You will see a Blue Arrow on a gatepost pointing along the farm road. You will now be following Blue Arrows until (4). Walk on along the road until you come to a gateway. (3) Follow Blue Arrow through gateway and continue walking (4) until you come to a gate with Yellow and Blue Arrows on it. You then turn right (without passing through gate) and FYA (see map). You will now be Following Yellow Arrows until (12). (5) Now go on until you come to a gate on your left. FYA through gate and walk on keeping the stone wall on your right. (6) Follow the field round passing by (7) Beckbury Hill Fort on your left and going on until (8) you come to a gate in the corner of the field. Go through gate, (9) and in a clump of trees you will see a large stone monument. This is known as Cromwells Seat. It is believed that at the time of the Dissolution of the Monasteries in 1539, Thomas Cromwell sat at that spot and watched the great Abbey of Hailes being pulled down. Just down through the trees you will find a post with an arrow on it. FYA and cross the field in the direction of the arrow. (9a) As you cross the field you can see a hole in the bank on your left. This looks like a burial chamber entrance, but is just below some modern ruins. It is unlikely to be the end of one of the secret tunnels coming from the old monastery. It is more likely to be a Shepherds Hole, a place where a shepherd could get out of the wind and cold. (10) Go through the gate into the next field. FYA. Cross field to next gate (11). Go through the gate and again cross this field to the next gate/stile. (12) This gate/stile leads into a lane. Go into the lane and turn right following the sign saying 'Hailes Abbey 1.5km'. (13) Keep on walking down this pleasant lane, passing the entrance to Hayles Fruit Farm on your left. Keep on walking until you reach Hailes Abbey. (14) Hailes Abbey is a must for you to look round. Leave yourselves 45 minutes to an hour for a good look round this most interesting site and museum. Hailes Abbey is owned by the National Trust but is maintained and run by the Department of the Environment.

This ends the first half of this walk.

— STUMPS CROSS —

24

STUMPS CROSS to HAILES ABBEY
Walkabout
Time: 3hrs (including visit to Abbey ruins)
Distance: 3km

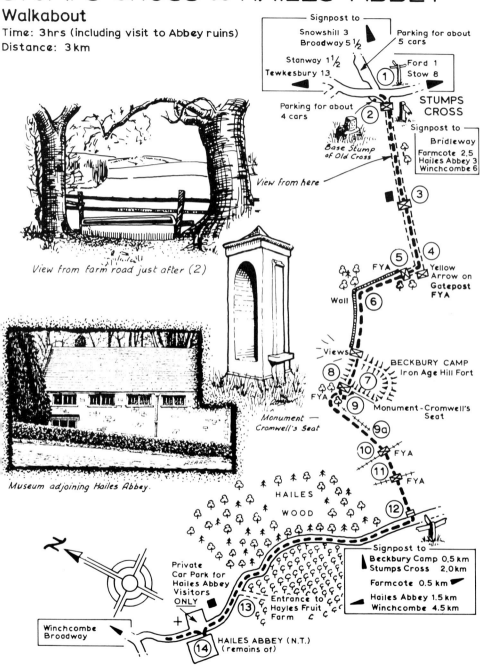

Signpost to
Snowshill 3
Broadway 5 ½
Parking for about 5 cars

Stanway 1½
Tewkesbury 13
Ford 1
Stow 8

① STUMPS CROSS

Parking for about 4 cars

②
Signpost to
Bridleway
Farmcote 2.5
Hailes Abbey 3
Winchcombe 6

Base Stump of Old Cross

View from here

③

④

⑤ FYA
Yellow Arrow on Gatepost FYA

Wall ⑥

View from farm road just after (2)

Views
⑧ FYA

BECKBURY CAMP
Iron Age Hill Fort
⑦

⑨ Monument - Cromwell's Seat

Monument — Cromwell's Seat

⑨a

⑩ FYA

⑪ FYA

Museum adjoining Hailes Abbey.

HAILES
WOOD ⑫

Private Car Park for Hailes Abbey Visitors ONLY ■

⑬ Entrance to Hayles Fruit Farm

Signpost to
Beckbury Camp 0.5 km
Stumps Cross 2.0km
Farmcote 0.5 km
Hailes Abbey 1.5 km
Winchcombe 4.5km

Winchcombe Broadway

⑭ HAILES ABBEY (N.T.) (remains of)

25

The Hailes Abbey to Stumps Cross Walkabout

Second half of the walk.
Come out of Hailes Abbey and turn left passing a little church on your right. Walk on until you come to a T junction, turn right here and walk on until (16) you come to a signpost pointing down a farm track across a concrete yard. The sign points the way to 'Wood Stanway 1.5km, Stanway 3km'. Follow this sign and walk along the track, then (17) go through the gate and where the track forks take the left-hand route. (18) When the track runs out keep walking on in the same direction with the trees and then hedges to your left and the field to your right (19) until you come to a gate at the end of the field. Go through the gate and walk round the next field in a clockwise direction passing an orchard on the way, on your left. At this point you should be able to see Didbrooks Church of St. George. Carry on walking and (20) go through the next gate you come to and cross the field to the next gate. (21) Go through the gate and walk on till you come to a gate which leads on to a village road. (22) Pass through the gate and you are now in the village of Wood Stanway. Walk on down the road and you will see a pipe and tap coming out of what looks like a monument. It is in fact the old water supply to the village from the 1920-30's. It was fed from higher up the hill, possibly a spring at the head of a tributary of the River Isbourne. A point of interest - the river Isbourne is the only river in the area that flows directly north. However, walk on to the end of the road and turn left and in a few paces turn right at the road juction. At this junction a sign saying 'Hailes Abbey 2km' pointing the way from where you have just come. (23) Continue walking, ignoring the lane on your right, through the village (24) until you see a Bridleway sign pointing into a farm yard. This sign shows 'Stumps Cross 1.5km, Temple Guiting 5km'. It is now possible to Follow Yellow Arrows right back to the starting point. (25) Walk through the farm yard and over the farm gate into the field and walk on to another gate on which you will see a Yellow Arrow. (26) FYA over gate and head across the field in the direction of the arrow, till you come to another gate with an arrow on it. All the way from the farm you are steadily climbing and the views are getting more interesting all the time. (27) FYA over the gate and head up the field towards another farm. You are now at Lower Coscombe. (28) Between the Farmhouse and the buildings you will see a gate. You are now 650ft above sea level. FYA over the gate and walk on through the farm yard. (29) Keep right and go through the next gate and FYA on to Private Road. Continue along this road until it joins the main B4077. (30) When you reach the main road you will see a sign pointing the way you have come indicating 'Wood Stanway 1.5km, Stanway 2.5km'. Now turn right and start walking up the main road back to Stumps Cross and your car.

The Church of St George in Didbrook, Glos.

HAILES ABBEY to STUMPS CROSS

Walkabout

Time: 2 hrs
Distance: 3.5 km

Signpost to ──
Stanway 1½
Tewkesbury 13

Snowshill 3
Broadway 5½

Parking for about 5 cars

Private Road

Stow 8
Ford 1

Stumps Cross

Farm Buildings

30

FYA 28
Field
27

FYA
29

FYA
Lower Coscombe Farm

Bridleway to
Stumps Cross 1.5 km
Temple Guiting 5 km

Signpost to
Wood Stanway 1.5 km
Stanway 2.5 km

25 Field 26 Field
FYA

24
FYA Field FYA
White Arrow on Green

Signpost to
Hailes Abbey 2 km
Winchcombe 5 km

23
Hamlet of
Wood Stanway

Amendments 1991
The FYA at (28) now takes you round
the farm buildings instead of through
them and on to the private road just
ahead of the gate at (29)

22

Field

21

idbrook
hurch

Field

20

Field

19

Field

*Site of the
old water supply of the 1920-30's
in Wood Stanway.*

18

17

Private Car Park
for Hailes Abbey
Visitors ONLY

Winchcombe
Broadway

16

15 14

HAILES ABBEY (N.T.)
(remains of)

Original culvert under Hailes Abbey

FYA	Follow Yellow Arrow
	Stile
	Gate
---	Walkers Track
++++	Fence
	Stone Wall
	Hedgerow or row of Bushes
	Roadway or Lane
	Track or Driveway

This Drawing is Not To Scale

27

Sunday Afternoon Walks for all the family:-

Wild Fowl Trust, Slimbridge
Denfurlong Farm Trail, Lower Chedworth, Nr. Northleach
Cotswold Farm Park, Guiting Power
Cotswold Wildlife Park,Burford, Oxon
Westonbirt Arboretum, Tetbury
Broadway Tower Country Park, Broadway, Worcs
Hidcote Manor Gardens, Hidcote Bartrim, Nr Chipping Campden
Sezincote Garden, Moreton in Marsh
Dyrham Park, Nr Bath, Avon
Barnsley House Garden, Barnsley
Kiftsgate Court Garden, Chipping Campden
Lydney Park Gardens, Lydney
Westbury Court Gardens, Westbury on Severn
Batsford Park Arboretum, Moreton in Marsh
Sudeley Castle and Gardens, Winchcombe

For those of our Readers who are keenly interested in walks and walking and wish to
further their experiences, the following addresses may be useful:-

Ramblers' Association

The Ramblers' Association is the
national organisation for all who enjoy
walking in the countryside.

Nationally the RA acts as a pressure
group, lobbying Ministers about issues
of concern to walkers, commenting on official reports and proposed new legislation,
giving evidence to official Committees and briefing sympathetic MPs and Peers for
debates in Parliament.

Locally the RA keeps a constant watch on rights of way, and examines closely any
proposals for closures and diversions. Many RA Groups carry out practical work on the
paths by organising clearance parties and waymarking projects to make paths easier to
follow.

Join the Ramblers' Association and work with 40,000 others to support the national
organisation working for all who enjoy walking in the countryside. Membership entitles
you to join in the activities of a nearby Group as well as many other benefits. Further
details from:
The Ramblers' Association, 1/5 Wandsworth Road, London SW8 2LJ.

The Cotswold Voluntary Warden Service.
address:-
Head Warden,
Cotswolds A.O.N.B.,
c/o County Planning Department,
Shire Hall,
Gloucester.

Broadway Tower, on a spot known as Broadway Beacon on the edge of the Cotswolds, was built by the Earl of Coventry for his Countess who wondered if a fire built on this spot could be seen from their family home at Croome Court. It could be, so the tower was built. — Just one of the many interesting places to visit in the area. There are many more and we suggest you contact one of many Tourist Information Centres scattered throughout the Cotswolds for further information.

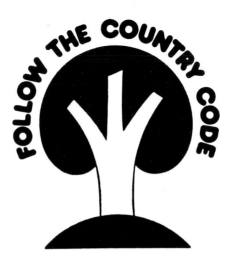

THE TEN COMMANDMENTS - COUNTRY STYLE

The Code is a set of ten reminders based on common sense — and common failings.   So when in the country please remember:

Guard against all risk of fire
Fasten all gates
Keep dogs under proper control
Keep to the paths across farmland
Avoid damaging fences, hedges and walls
Leave no litter
Safeguard water supplies
Protect wildlife, wild plants and trees
Go carefully on country roads
Respect the life of the countryside

Thank you

KEEP BRITAIN TIDY

Keep Britain Tidy Group
Bostel House,
37 West Street,
Brighton. BN1 2RE

INDEX

LOOK Out! for
our other products

Post Cards
Prints
Driveabout Packs
Post Card Packs
Cotswold Driveabout
Cotswold Driveabout - South
Calendars
and other drives and walks books

REARDON & SON

PUBLISHERS

56 Upper Norwood Street
Leckhampton
Cheltenham, Glos. GL53 0DU

Phone 231800
S.T.D. 0242
